Explore the Outdoors

Hunting

Have Fun, Be Smart

By Jack Weaver

Rosen Publishing Group, Inc.
New York

To the volunteer hunter/trapper education instructors throughout North America, who dedicate their time and energy to educate youth in the fundamentals of hunting and trapping

Published in 2000 by The Rosen Publishing Group, Inc.
29 East 21st Street, New York, NY 10010

Copyright © 2000 by The Rosen Publishing Group, Inc.

First Edition

Weaver, Jack.
    Hunting : have fun, be smart / Jack Weaver.
       p. cm. — (Explore the outdoors)
    Includes bibliographical references and index.
    Summary: Introduces the sport of hunting, its history, equipment, skills, techniques, how to get started, and firearm safety.
      ISBN 0-8239-3167-6
      1. Hunting—Juvenile literature. [1. Hunting.] I. Title. II. Series.
    799.2—dc21
    SK35.5 .W43 2000
                                                           00-021285

Manufactured in the United States of America

Contents

Introduction   4

1   Hunting History   8

2   Equipment You Need   15

3   The Way of the Hunter   25

4   A Word About Safety   31

5   Let's Get Started!   35

6   Developing Skills   41

7   Hunting Pros and Cons   47

Glossary   52   For Further Reading   60

Resources   58   Index   62

Introduction

Imagine slipping through the woods in the predawn darkness. Your destination is a wooded ridge that presides over a shallow mountain valley. A crystal stream teeming with brook trout winds its way through a beaver meadow below the ridge.

You make your way through thick stands of tag alder and aspen with their mint green leaves just beginning to open in the surge of warm spring air. The reek of swamp mud assails your nostrils as you cross the breast of a small buffer dam below the beavers' main holding. Here the sharply chiseled ends of brush and small trees the beavers cut for food threaten to trip you or punch a painful hole through a boot. When you reach the wooded ridge the pale light of dawn seeps over the eastern mountains.

Suddenly you are startled by a chorus of young barred owls, their loud crazy hooting erupting out of the gloom to your left. Then from a distant ridge comes the deep hollow rhythm of a great horned owl. You are about to continue your climb up the ridge when suddenly the whole valley echoes with the challenging gobble of a wild turkey, coming from right up the hill in front of you. Now you must get closer to the roosting bird without flushing it. You move cautiously in the eerie light of dawn, acutely aware of the crunch of leaves and the snap of twigs underfoot.

Then another gobble erupts from across a little ravine to your right. Your bird answers with a loud reverberating challenge. Still another gobbler answers from across the beaver dam where you just came from. Both gobblers on your side return the challenge. Red streaks light the eastern horizon. Soon the sun will be up and the birds will fly off their roost. You must find a place to hide quickly.

Choosing a spot that affords a fairly good view up the hill, you settle down with your back next to a large hemlock and adjust your camouflage face net and gloves, then get your turkey call ready and prepare to wait. Several minutes go by, and then you hear the beat of heavy wings and the crack of twigs breaking as several large birds fly down from the trees. This gobbler has a harem of hens. Your job just got harder. The turkey across the beaver meadow stops gobbling. He must be on the ground. Your bird gobbles once more before you hear him fly down from his roost. When he lands the bird issues another challenge. By the sound, you judge him to be about a hundred yards or so in front of you. Then he is answered by the gobbler to your right. This bird sounds farther away but you guess he is on the ground too and that the intervening terrain now muffles the sound.

You pick up your call and give a couple of soft clucks, trying to sound like an interested hen. You are rewarded by answering gobbles from the bird in front and the one to the right. Now you make two soft yelps. There is an explosion of sound as the gobbler up the hill answers from about half the distance he was before. Later the turkey to your right answers, and it sounds as though he is closer, but moving down the ravine, circling behind.

The calling continues back and forth. Both gobblers are just out of sight about fifty yards away. Then you see movement. To your left, two hens are coming in from an angle, clucking softly and stopping occasionally to scratch or pick something from the ground. You dare not move. Hens are not in season. Only bearded

5

gobblers may be taken during the spring. You freeze, hoping they won't spot you and give the alarm.

Suddenly the turkey behind you gobbles loudly. You can hear him walking in the leaves and dragging his wings in full strut. You know he's close. Really close! But you can't turn around because of the hens. Your heart is pounding so hard you fear the turkeys can hear it. There is more movement up the hill directly in front of you as a huge shape looms from the shadows. It's the first gobbler, his tail fanned, his chest fluffed out, his beard dragging the ground between his legs as he struts forward. Still you can't move. You're using a shotgun, and the maximum effective range is thirty yards. This bird is just out of

range. The shotgun is resting on your knees, and attempting to raise it to a firing position would scare the turkeys. These are the sharpest-eyed creatures in the woods.

You wait, hoping the big gobbler and the hens will step behind a tree long enough for you to bring your gun to bear. The other gobbler *is close, too—you hear him circling around from behind. Will he spot you first? Will you get your shot? Or will the birds flush, putting trees and brush between you and them so fast it will make your eyes blink?*

Whether hunting for grouse and woodcock in the eastern woodlands, working pheasants behind a pair of English setters in the Great Plains, shivering in a waterfowl blind along the Atlantic seaboard, gunning for doves in Texas, stalking deer, elk, or moose in the Rocky Mountains, or just plunking for squirrels, people hunt for the unique challenges each sport offers. Hunting satisfies the need to be outdoors in a different way than hiking or camping. Hunting requires the mastery of certain fundamental skills such as marksmanship, woods lore, wildlife knowledge, and tracking. Hunters also need a sense of camaraderie and a high level of outdoor ethics, especially a sense of fair chase. Hunting is an exercise of the primal survival traits the human race was born with. Hunting is a unique privilege that was hard earned, as you will learn in the next chapter. And the hunter is rewarded by finally sitting down to enjoy a roast of venison, a brace of ducks, or a dinner with friends of whatever wild game he or she was fortunate enough to bring home.

Hunting is not for the fainthearted, nor for the careless. It is a rugged sport that demands a high degree of integrity and responsibility on the part of those who partake of its challenges and rewards. Hunting demands respect for the land, respect for the game you hunt, respect for others, and even respect for yourself. For those who will accept those demands, adventures that will provide cherished memories for a lifetime await.

Hunting History

Hunting has been around almost as long as humans have. From the first prehistoric hunters until fairly recently, human beings have hunted for one primary reason: food for survival. Within the last few hundred years, however, hunting for sport has also become more common. In this book we will focus mainly on the kinds of game and methods of hunting that are popular in the Americas.

The Colonial Era

It was mostly poor immigrants who populated the American colonies. In the beginning there was little industry, and farming in the forest was difficult at best. But the continent was teeming with wildlife and natural resources. Because wild game was needed for food, the colonists decided that this bounty should belong to everyone and not just the landowners, as was the case in Europe.

Unfortunately, wildlife and other natural resources were mistakenly thought to be inexhaustible. As pioneers pushed farther into the interior, an explosion of industry followed. Railroads and more modern firearms were soon to wreak havoc

Early Europe

The ancestors of today's hunters had much to contend with. Although wild game such as wild boar, bears, deer, partridges and rabbits abounded in Europe during medieval times, wild game belonged to the king and his lords

and ladies; if you were a commoner, you were not permitted to hunt for food. The penalty for poaching was death. In England, for example, the king's gamekeepers even used leghold traps to catch poachers, who were then slain on the spot—even for killing a rabbit! That is one of the reasons Robin Hood was an outlaw. He and his band of merry men lived off the king's game.

with America's wildlife resources. Rather than merely providing meat for frontier kitchens, hunting wildlife suddenly became a highly competitive industry. Armed with mass-produced firearms, market hunters shipped boxcar loads of wild game to eastern markets.

Even before the turn of the twentieth century, America's natural resources were quickly becoming depleted. In the West, the buffalo and beaver were all but gone. In the East, elk, furbearers, large predators, waterfowl, and flocks of passenger pigeons, so numerous their migrations darkened the sky, were also gone. Whitetail deer were so scarce that when a deer track was found whole communities would get in their buggies and drive out to see it. Flocks of wild turkeys, grouse, and even black bears were making a last stand in a few remote mountain ranges. Even the rugged hills of the Allegheny Mountains, once covered with virgin stands of giant oak, chestnut, white pine, and hemlock, were reduced to eroded, fire-swept ridges by the logger's axe. But by the late 1800s a new breed of hunter was emerging on the American scene. They called themselves sportsmen.

The Role of the Sportsman

In the early days of sport hunting, sportsmen were mostly people of influence. They lamented the loss of the wild game they loved to hunt and began to politick for change. They formed sportsmen's protective associations, and as a result of their lobbying, individual states began to form wildlife agencies. Laws establishing seasons and bag limits on wildlife were enacted, and game wardens were hired to enforce those laws on behalf of all the people. These were not popular laws,

and many game wardens were killed trying to enforce them.

By the late 1930s, most state game agencies began to hire wildlife biologists, and a new era of scientific wildlife management was born. Modern wildlife management has been and still is a hard-fought battle against those who would destroy wildlife habitats through pollution and expanded development. Sportsmen and sportswomen have led the fight for wildlife conservation. This may initially seem like a contradiction, for sportsmen and sportswomen do indeed hunt. However, they were the first to set limits that would protect wildlife against extinction. The sportsmen and sportswomen of America help pay the bill for wildlife management through hunting license fees, special excise taxes on hunting and fishing equipment, and donations of their time and energy to help wildlife agencies develop wildlife habitats.

Because of the wildlife management efforts of American sportsmen and sportswomen, North America is once again teeming with wildlife. Most wild game species are again plentiful, and in some cases abundant. Still others, like the buffalo and bald eagle, have been rescued from the brink of extinction. Although there are more species on the endangered species list than ever before, very few are game species. Nor are they endangered because of sport hunting. Habitat losses due to urbanization and chemical pollution are the key factors in the decline of wildlife species today.

Actually, sport hunting in North America has never been better. Although carefully managed by state game departments, big game of all types is abundant. Upland game birds are plentiful. Waterfowl hunting is very carefully monitored and managed by both the U.S. Fish and Wildlife Service and state wildlife agencies, but today most species of waterfowl are plentiful. With the exception of the eastern farming communities, small game hunting is relatively good, especially woodland species.

The Spectrum of Sport Hunting

Today's sportsmen and sportswomen are willing to travel long distances to pursue their sport. Eastern hunters travel west in pursuit of Rocky Mountain elk, bighorn sheep, mountain goats, antelope, mule deer and mountain lions. Hunters gunning for ring-necked pheasants pursue their sport in the Great Plains. Waterfowl hunters pursue ducks and geese in the pothole country of the Midwest or along the major flyways. Brown bears, grizzlies, caribou, and Dall sheep are found in Alaska. Northern whitetails, caribou, and

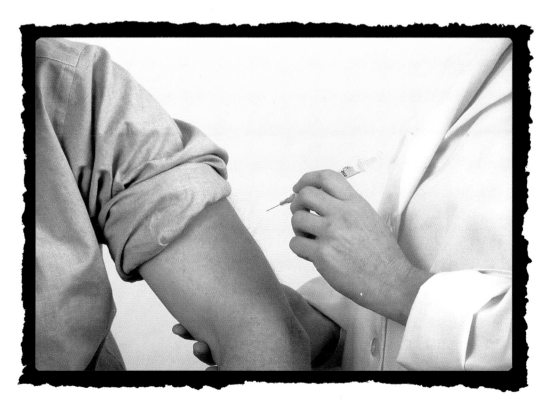

moose are hunted in the Canadian provinces, while big racked whitetails are sought in Texas, along with wild razor-backed hogs.

Nowadays more hunters than ever before are packing their bags and traveling to ever more exotic places. Hunting trips are routinely booked to nearly all parts of the world, including South America, Asia, Australia, Russia, Africa, and the Arctic, in pursuit of everything from big cats to musk ox. But one doesn't just hop on a plane and fly off to wild new places. Passports and visas are needed. So are lots of immunization shots. Ouch! In addition, a reputable outfitter who is familiar with such things as endangered species and importation laws is a must. Good outfitters will not only make your trip run smoother and know how to find the game when you get there, but they can also keep you out of foreign jails.

For Starters

For the beginner, however, try starting a little closer to home. For example, try hunting for rabbits or squirrels on a nearby woodlot, farm, or ranch. As a beginner, this will allow you to become familiar with simpler firearms such as the common .22 caliber rifle. Dove or upland game bird hunting is also a sport for beginners who need to put some hunting experience under their belts before venturing into the big woods in pursuit of more challenging game. Before you can get started, however, you will need to know what is available in terms of equipment.

2 Equipment You Need

Choosing the proper equipment can be especially daunting to the beginner. Consider a shotgun, for example. Should you choose a mule-kicking 10 gauge, a 12 gauge, a 16 gauge, 20 gauge, 28 gauge, or the snappy little 4.10, which is really a caliber and not a gauge? Next, do you want a semiautomatic, a pump action, bolt action, hinged action, double barrel, or single barrel? After deciding what type of shotgun you want, you may choose from several brands, depending on your budget. Of course, you should choose a properly choked barrel or barrels for your shotgun. Then come the decisions about ammunition. What size shot? What type of shot? What brand of shot? Or maybe you want rifled slugs instead? Actually it all depends on what you intend to hunt. Understanding some simple basics helps.

Choosing a Firearm

The first major choice the beginner must face is the type of game he or she would like to hunt. The firearm depends entirely upon the game you intend to hunt. Actually, there are only two types of sporting arms—rifles and shotguns. The difference is inside the barrel. A rifle barrel has grooves cut inside. These

rifle

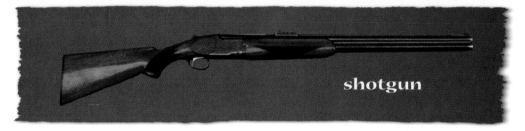

shotgun

grooves twist around the length of the rifle's barrel. Their purpose is to cause the bullet to spin or spiral much like the spin a quarterback puts on a football when he throws it. This causes the bullet to travel farther and be more accurate.

A shotgun's barrel, on the other hand, is perfectly smooth inside. Unlike a rifle, which fires one bullet at a time, a shotgun generally shoots a charge of small round pellets called shot. This is why shotgun size is measured by gauge, which relates to the size of the shot charge that a particular shotgun is capable of handling. A rifle is measured by caliber, which is a measurement of the diameter of the bullet it can fire.

Of course there is always an exception to every rule, and as we mentioned earlier, the little 4.10 shotgun is actually a caliber. Generally, however, the smaller the gauge, the bigger the diameter of the shotgun's barrel and the larger the shot charge it can fire. For rifles the opposite is true. The smaller the caliber, the smaller the bullet a particular rifle will fire. So a .22 caliber rifle and a 20-gauge shotgun are good for beginners because they are easier to handle and have less recoil.

Ammunition

Ammunition must be handled carefully and with respect for what it can do. A little .22 bullet can travel up to a mile and a half. High-powered rifle and even pistol ammunition may travel much farther. Although most shotgun ammunition is designed for shorter distances—generally under fifty yards— the shot pattern can travel much farther. In addition, bullets do not always stop when they hit something. Often they will pierce through their target and continue on. Shooters must be aware of these simple ballistics and be sure there is a proper backstop behind their targets in order to protect other people and property.

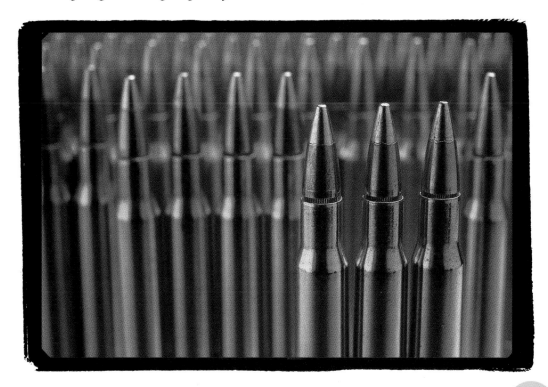

The type of ammunition you buy will depend on the firearm and the quarry, or game, you intend to hunt. In the case of shotgun ammo, the size of the shot loads, meaning how big the pellets are inside the shell, will also depend on the size of your quarry. Size nine to seven and a half are generally used for quail, doves, or grouse. The carton the ammunition comes in will usually explain what game the shot size is effective for. Again, depending on the game you are gunning for, you might choose lead, tin, bismuth, or steel shot pellets. Also, be sure to match the caliber of rifle ammunition with the caliber of the firearm. Rifle ammunition is manufactured with different power loads and bullet tips designed for specific game species. Check with a reputable sporting goods dealer who deals with firearms and ammunition to purchase the correct match.

A good sharp knife is also necessary equipment for the hunter. In the case of knives, bigger is not always better. A knife with a blade no longer than four inches is plenty. Buy a brand-name knife that is known for holding a keen edge. A dull knife is useless. When considering knives, look for a folding knife with a locking blade. A folding knife is safer and easier to carry, and the blade should lock in place when extended to prevent it from snapping shut on your fingers.

Dress for Success

There is lots of outdoor clothing on the market for today's hunters. For certain types of hunting, some states require specific amounts of bright orange to be visible at all times. Before you purchase clothing, check the hunting regulations for the area you intend to hunt. But whether you are looking for the latest in camouflage design or the brightest safety clothing, remember that you are going outdoors. Dress for the weather. Most hunting is generally done during the fall and winter. In northern climates layered clothing is best. The outer garment should be water resistant or waterproof. In warmer climates clothing that breathes will allow a free flow of air and help to prevent overheating. This type of clothing will also dry faster should you encounter a surprise shower or fall into a swamp. Generally speaking, blue jeans are not the best clothing to wear in the outdoors, especially when hunting. Good boots, however, are a must. Purchase the best you can afford. Waterproof is best, especially in colder weather. Hunting boots should extend over the ankles for good support in unstable terrain. They should have a rugged sole for traction and wear. You will probably be out in all kinds of weather, and your boots should be comfortable yet rugged

enough to handle it. Your feet are your transportation. If you treat your feet well, they will treat you well. There is nothing worse than wet, cold, and sore feet.

Maps

No hunter should be without a good topographical map of the area he or she plans to hunt and a compass or a global positioning system (GPS). Local topographical maps can usually be purchased at sporting goods stores. These maps give detailed information about everything from roads, trails, streams, and buildings to terrain elevation and the types of vegetation you will encounter. Purchase a good compass or GPS and learn to use them. Instructions come with both. A compass may be purchased for a few dollars and should always be used as a backup for a GPS unit anyway. A global positioning system is a handheld computer that works with a navigational satellite and costs considerably more than a compass.

Hunting License

Finally, don't forget your hunting license. Different states have their own requirements for purchasing a hunting license, including resident and nonresident requirements. Other considerations include age requirements for junior licenses, whether a junior hunter must be accompanied by an adult, and hunter education requirements for beginners. Depending on the state where you intend to hunt, there may also be a variety of required licenses, such as big or small game tags or specific species stamps, to purchase. Be sure to check with your state's wildlife agency for details on licensing requirements.

You're Losing Me With All These Requirements . . .

Actually it isn't as bad as it may seem. For starters, you may be able to borrow a firearm from a family member or a friend. Be sure to have a borrowed firearm checked by someone knowledgeable about guns to be sure it is safe and that it functions properly. Ammunition isn't all that expensive, and most of the clothes used for hunting may also be worn for other outdoor pursuits such as hiking, camping, or fishing. One of the really neat things about hunting is that you may pursue the sport in one fashion or another all year round. If the hunting season isn't open, go hiking. Walk around the area you intend to hunt and become familiar with the lay of the land, what animals live there, and where their food sources are located. That is called scouting and you can do it anytime. If most of the wild land near you is posted against trespassing, get permission from the landowner first. You'll

Your Survival Kit

It is also a good idea to purchase or put together a survival kit. Commercial survival kits may be purchased at most sporting goods stores for a reasonable fee. A good survival kit should contain some basic first aid items, a whistle, material for making a shelter, a small flashlight, extra food, and fire starting materials, including waterproof matches.

find more on this subject in chapter 5. If you don't have ready access to huntable land, remember that half the fun of hunting is learning about wildlife. Check the lists in the back of this book for ideas on how to do that. Meanwhile, get outdoors as much as possible and start looking for wildlife. Even the biggest city has wild animals living there. Check out the park, vacant lots, stream banks, and marshes. If there is grass, trees, or water, there is wildlife. Roll over a stone or two. You may be surprised at what you find. Be careful, but don't forget to have fun!

3 The Way of the Hunter

Remember the hunting scene in the Introduction? Well, one method of hunting game involves calling your quarry within range, and generally that means up close and personal. This chapter will touch on these and other methods of getting closer to your game.

Calling Your Game

Many species of game may be hunted by calling. In the case of turkeys this means trying to imitate a hen in the spring or a lost member of the flock during the fall. Ducks and geese are generally called within the close range necessary for shotguns by trying to imitate the feeding sounds of other waterfowl. Still other game may be called in close by imitating the fighting sounds of male rivals during breeding season. Bucks, for example, may be called within bow shot by rattling antlers and with the use of a grunt call. Bull elk and moose sometimes respond to the challenging bugles of their kind with explosive action. Predators such as coyotes and foxes may be called by imitating their quarry's distress calls or the distress calls of one of their young. Crows may also be called in this fashion, and the list doesn't end here. Although anyone can do it, learning to call game successfully takes considerable practice and patience. However, it is one of the most exciting and satisfying methods of hunting there is.

Stalking

Perhaps the most common method of hunting is stalking. This involves walking slowly and quietly through the woods looking for game. The key here is to know where your quarry is likely to be at any given time. You wouldn't want to be stalking through the high country if all the elk are in the lowlands. This is where preseason scouting and knowing your quarry come in handy. If you are after deer, for example, you will need to learn their feeding habits, where their feeding areas are, and when they move into or away from their feeding areas. You must also know where they are likely to shelter during stormy weather and where their bedding or resting areas are. For the restless hunter, stalking is a good alternate technique.

Stand Hunting

Stand hunting is popular today, but it can be misleading for the beginner. Hunting from a stand, whether it is a portable tree stand, some type of permanent stand, or just a favorite spot, depends upon the natural movements of wildlife to be successful. Animal movement patterns change over time because the woods are in a constant state of flux. Just because someone got their deer on a particular stand for the past ten years doesn't mean that spot will continue to produce. Again, scouting the area you intend to hunt is a must. Look for game trails, buck rubs or scrapes, droppings,

and the availability of food. You'll learn more about tree stands in the next chapter.

Driving Game

For certain types of hunting, driving game is by far the most productive method. Driving game generally involves several hunters cooperating together, although small drives can be done by as few as two hunters. When driving, a hunting party is divided into two groups—drivers and watchers. It is the drivers' job to get the game moving by traveling through the woods in a sort of skirmish line. The watchers are positioned at strategic points where the game is expected to go. Obviously, this takes a good deal of cooperation on the part of everyone involved and requires some serious safety considerations. But it is an effective technique, especially for whitetailed deer.

Other Methods

Hunting from blinds and using bait to attract animals are other methods hunters use to take game. Blinds are simple shelters constructed to conceal a hunter while he or she waits for game. Blinds can be used for most types of game, but the most popular quarries for blind hunting are waterfowl, turkeys, deer, or bear. Sometimes bait is used in connection with a blind to attract animals to a certain spot or within range. Both hunting from blinds and the use of bait are prohibited when hunting certain species, or altogether prohibited, depending on the state or country you are hunting in. Check the hunting regulations for the area where you plan to hunt.

Perhaps one of the most enjoyable methods of hunting involves the use of hunting dogs. There is nothing quite like experiencing a pair of setters on point, listening to the honey-tongued bark of a beagle or the mournful cry of a coon hound striking a trail along the edge of a cornfield. Most breeds of hunting dogs are a joy to keep and often make good house pets to boot. There are breeds for almost every conceivable type of game. What type of dog you pick will depend on the type of game you enjoy hunting the most.

Perhaps the two sports in the hunting arena that are enjoying the most growth are archery hunting and muzzle loading. A tremendous amount of new archery equipment has been developed in recent years, and the sport has become one of the most popular of all the hunting sports. Generally, archery hunting is done during October and November when the weather is still mild and the woods are alive with the beauty of autumn. Archery hunting is a quiet, solitary sport that involves staking out a deer trail in a breeding area, blending into the colorful fall foliage with camouflage clothing and a tree stand, and waiting for that big racked buck to come within range. Or, as we mentioned earlier, the hunter might try rattling a buck within range. Some archers hunt everything from small game to grizzlies with a bow and arrow. If you want to be challenged, this may be just the sport for you.

Muzzle loading is hunting with black powder firearms. Muzzle loading, like the name implies, involves loading one shot at a time right down the muzzle with a ramrod. Some states allow hunting with modern in-line muzzle loaders while others only permit primitive cap and ball or flintlock ignition systems. But when hunting with a muzzle loader, the old adage "keep your powder dry" still applies!

These are only a few of the popular techniques used in hunting today. Whatever technique you choose, be sure one important element is always present: fair chase. In order for hunting to remain a viable sport, the quarry must always have a fair chance of survival. Considering the modern hunting equipment available today, that statement may sound like a misnomer, but we must keep in mind that the extraordinary traits of wild things are such that they still maintain the upper hand. This is why wildlife agencies regulate the types of equipment and the methods that may be used for hunting. The idea of fair chase is what makes sport hunting a sport.

4 A Word About Safety

Learning to hunt is a lot like learning to drive a car. There is no place for a reckless or an irresponsible person behind the wheel of an automobile, and the same holds true for hunting. Irresponsible actions with a firearm can lead to death or cause serious injury to people and property. For this reason almost every state requires first-time hunters to complete a hunter education course sponsored by the state's wildlife agency. An identification card is issued to each successful graduate. This card must then be shown when purchasing a hunting license.

Today, hunter education courses are being standardized throughout the country. Qualified volunteers, under the supervision of a state wildlife agency, teach the course. Courses generally require a minimum of ten hours or more to complete.

Hunter Education Courses

Today's hunter education courses include handling and safety, ammunition, firearm safety in the home, hunter responsibility, game identification, survival, first aid, ethics, landowner relations, game laws, archery, muzzle loading, and much, much more.

Most courses teach marksmanship and shooting fundamentals by offering live firing on a range under the supervision of a qualified range master. Many also offer mock hunts that walk the student through actual field courses. Some states are now offering home study courses—some with CD interactive scenarios. The purpose of home study is to allow busy students the opportunity to complete the academic portion of the course at home. After successfully completing the written portion of the course, he or she would then have to complete the practical, hands-on portion under the supervision of course instructors.

To find out how to register for a hunter education course, contact your state wildlife agency, local sportsman's club, or inquire at gun shops and sporting goods stores in your area.

The Basic Rules

Actually, hunter safety, like any safety issue, is simply applying common sense when in the field. Hunter education identifies and then clarifies these safety issues for the beginner and experienced hunter alike. Three basic rules of firearm safety sum it up best. Plant them firmly in your mind, and follow them as though they were written in stone. That way, you can truly have fun and be smart!

Tree Stand Safety

Tree stand safety is one of the leading issues in hunting circles today. On a nationwide average, more people are

Three Basic Rules for Hunting Safety

1. Treat every firearm as if it were loaded! Every firearm must be treated with respect. Assume every gun is loaded until you personally look into the action (those parts that load and fire a gun) to be sure it is not.

2. Always keep the muzzle pointed in a safe direction! The muzzle is the business end of a firearm. Always keep the muzzle of your firearm pointed in a safe direction—away from others. That way, should the gun be set off accidentally, no one will be hurt.

3. Be sure of your target! Legal game is the only target any hunter should be shooting at. Double-check your target before you pull the trigger!

injured, some fatally, by falling from tree stands than through firearm mishaps. The majority of these accidents are preventable, and hunters should never go aloft without attaching themselves securely to the tree with a safety harness.

5 Let's Get Started!

So you want to go hunting? Well, okay. Deciding to do it is the first big step. Taking a hunter education course is the second. Having done that, you will need a firearm or bow and arrows. Assuming you've already decided on what you want to hunt and the type of gun you need, all that remains is to obtain your firearm.

There is one consideration, however: Are you of legal age to own firearms? Federal law prohibits persons under eighteen from purchasing or owning a shotgun or rifle, and prohibits those under twenty-one from purchasing or owning a handgun. (This federal law also prevails over state laws.) It isn't necessary to purchase a new sporting firearm if the price is a problem. Just about every gun shop sells both new and used firearms.

If you are purchasing a used firearm, be sure to purchase it from a reputable gun shop, one that checks used firearms thoroughly before offering them for resale to be sure they are working properly and are safe. If you are going to borrow one from a relative, neighbor, or friend, be sure to have it checked by someone familiar with that type of firearm to be sure it is safe before shooting it. More than one gun has exploded in the shooter's hands because someone accidentally left a cleaning patch inside the barrel. Especially check the safety mechanism (the part that blocks the trigger from firing prematurely) to be sure that it is working properly.

Mentoring

Traditionally, hunting is a sport that has been handed down from father to son as a part of a family's traditions. Today that has changed. For one thing, more women are becoming involved in hunting and other forms of outdoor recreation. For many reasons, hunting is not being pursued as actively as it once was, which is good for those who do hunt because more hunting opportunities are opening up. These are great times to be hunting! But it may be a little difficult for a beginner to find a mentor, especially since many parents no longer hunt.

Having a mentor to show you the way is important. It's sort of like having a pro baseball player teach you how to play ball. If your mom or dad is a nonhunter, let your friends and relatives who do hunt know that you are interested in learning about hunting. Often they will take you under their wing, so to speak. After all, they know the ropes and maybe even belong to a hunting camp somewhere. If your relatives don't hunt, ask friends of the family, but don't just grab anybody. Make sure your prospective mentor is a trustworthy and responsible person. Would you want someone who drives under the influence of drugs or alcohol to teach you about driving? I hope not! Anyway, you get the idea. If you have a local hunter's organization or shooting club that is active in your area, you might also check to see if they have youth programs or youth memberships. Then get involved with their group and group projects.

Other Options

For now, though, perhaps the very first thing you need to do is find out if hunting is really for you. Obviously you have an interest in outdoor recreation or you wouldn't be reading this book. But are you sure you are interested in hunting, or could your interest lean more toward camping, boating, fishing, hiking, or outdoor photography? Of course, you may combine any of those sports with hunting. The only way to find out, though, is to learn all you can about hunting first. There are lots of good books available about hunting. Check some out at the library. There are also several national magazines that feature hunting articles and stories. Also, check with your state wildlife agency. Most wildlife agencies publish a monthly conservation magazine that features hunting articles and articles about wildlife. All wildlife agencies have helpful books, brochures, and handouts. Most publish wildlife videos, which may be purchased inexpensively.

That's a good place to find a mentor for hunting and to learn to shoot as well.

Look Around

Finally, if you can, just get out in the woods. Walk around quietly and look for animals and animal signs. But be careful! Go someplace that is familiar to you at first so you don't get lost. Or go to a state park until you become used to making your way around in the outdoors. Go outside during different seasons of the year to see if you're really going to enjoy being out in all kinds of weather. Not everyone does. Also, choose your hiking companions wisely. It is not fun to be in the woods with someone who is bothered by insects, cobwebs, dirt, or snakes. You should learn what kinds of animals to stay away from—such as rattlesnakes, for example. Learn how to avoid areas where these critters may be found until you become comfortable dealing with such situations safely. If you respect the outdoors, the outdoors will respect you. Remember, respect is always earned.

Finally, always let someone know where you are going and when you plan to return. Give them a specific description of the area, such as the name of a hollow or canyon. That way, if you don't return within a reasonable time, they will know where to look or where to send search parties. After all, it is very easy to fall, break a leg, or sprain an ankle in the woods. Common sense and good judgment should always prevail.

6 Developing Skills

Marksmanship and other skills needed for hunting must be learned and developed, like any other sport. Hunting and shooting do not require a high degree of athletic ability. However, learning how to shoot requires an understanding of the fundamentals of marksmanship. As we already mentioned, taking a hunter education course will help get you started, but you still need to practice to become a skilled marksman. Target practice, therefore, becomes a necessary activity.

Starting Target Practice

Just setting out some tin cans or pinning up a paper target and blazing away is not the best way to learn. First, safety precautions must be taken. Remember that backstop we talked about to keep your bullets from traveling beyond the target? A beginner definitely needs the supervision of an experienced adult marksman. Joining a hunter's club is one way to accomplish this, since most clubs have some type of safe shooting facility available for their members. Another way might be to join a National Rifle Association shooting team. There you will get the valuable assistance of trained coaches.

For the competition-minded, there are lots of fun ways to develop and fine-tune those skills needed to become a successful hunter. Here are a few.

Small bore rifle (.22 caliber)

Competition in this category involves shooting at paper targets at different ranges and from different positions, such as lying down, sitting, and standing. Shooting may be done on either indoor or outdoor ranges. This is the best way for beginners to learn the basics of marksmanship.

High power rifle

These competitions are held at outdoor ranges. They may be very formal in terms of competition rules and conduct, or they may be casual, such as the type often conducted by local sportsmen and sportswomen. But whether formal or casual, the strict observance of range safety rules is always in order. High-power rifle contestants may shoot from a bench rest at paper targets at ranges anywhere from 100 yards to 1,000 yards or more. Some contests involve shooting at moving targets from off-hand standing positions. Some, such as the long-range competitions, require telescopic sights, while others may specify iron or open sights only.

Muzzle loader or black powder

These competitions are generally held with primitive-type firearms such as flintlock rifles. Many black powder shoots are gala events with the participants dressing in frontier or mountaineer clothing. Often shooting is done off-hand, but some matches are only done with heavy bench-rest target rifles. Novelty shooting is a hallmark of these events. One event involves shooting a soft lead ball at the edge of an axe that cuts the ball in two, hopefully, causing each piece to break a balloon on either side of the blade. Tomahawk and knife throwing are also a regular part of such competitions. Early American camps are usually set up at such events, and visitors are encouraged to tour and visit with the participants. This gives folks a real-life history lesson about early America that will not soon be forgotten.

Archery

Archery shooting may be done at a variety of targets from traditional bull's-eyes to Styrofoam replicas of game animals. Field archery courses involve shooting at replicas of game animals under actual field conditions. For example, contestants may walk through a wooded trail and shoot at targets set up at different ranges or even shoot from tree stands. Also, many archery shops now offer archery competitions that are actually done indoors. They simulate actual hunting situations with electronic machines that project hunting scenes on a target wall.

Trap and skeet shooting

This is traditional shotgun shooting at its best. With trap, shooters take up a position behind a low structure that houses a clay bird–throwing machine. When the shooter is ready, he or she yells "Pull!" and a clay disk is released at various speeds, angles, and height away from the shooter. The shooter who breaks the most wins. Skeet is a little different, in that a group of shooters stand in a semicircle. Two trap houses sit to the right and left of the shooters' positions. One is high and one low. Birds are thrown across the front of the shooters with combinations of singles, doubles or triples. The shooters' angles change as they rotate through the five firing positions. Shooting sporting clays where actual hunting situations are simulated is an ever more popular type of shotgun shooting competition. Clay bird traps are set up and hidden in a variety of actual field conditions, such as in a thick aspen wood or beside a pond. Each station simulates a different type of hunting situation. Various sizes of clay disks are used to imitate different types of game. Some bounce along the ground like a cottontail, others sail through the thick brush or come right at the shooter the way a grouse or dove might, and still others flush straight up like a pheasant or a mallard. This is the most realistic type of shotgun shooting that can be had, and it's fun!

Competition: Getting Involved

The National Rifle Association sponsors one of the best competitions for young people. The program is called Youth Hunter Education Challenge. Although the competition is open to single contestants, local sportsman clubs usually cosponsor the program. Regional, state, and national championships are then conducted annually. This competition involves outdoor rifle, shotgun, and archery shooting at simulated game animals under actual field conditions. The competition also involves a written test of hunter education principles, ethics, and a general knowledge of safety-related issues. A hunter safety trail offers contestants a hands-on test of game identification, survival skills, and compass orienteering.

Of course there are many other kinds of shooting sports competitions, including handguns, combat shooting, and others. Many state and national organizations are now offering special incentive programs for youths interested in hunting, including The National Wild Turkey Association's Jake's Day events. Youth Field Day events are offered in several states at local sportsmen clubs. Check the listings at the back of this book for Web sites that will help connect you with these and other skill-developing games and competitions.

7 Hunting Pros and Cons

"Hunting is cruel. It is deceitful. It is socially unjustifiable," says one of the nation's leading anti-hunting lobbies.

"Sportsmen and sportswomen are America's greatest conservationists," claims one of America's prominent conservation organizations.

In our society, people hold many different opinions regarding the treatment of animals. Some people object to any practice that involves the killing or using of animals. Others, such as those in one leading antihunting organization, claim that hunters take a heavy toll on endangered and threatened species.

However, when considering the pros and cons of hunting, it is important to get all the facts. In the case of hunters hurting endangered species, hunters are required to pay to protect threatened and endangered species. Hunters provide millions of dollars in the form of of special taxes on hunting equipment, licenses, and permits. This money is used to manage both protected and huntable species.. Animals such as the sea otter, the bald eagle, and the peregrine falcon have been brought back from the brink of extinction with the aid provided by this tax money.

Another important part of getting the facts is looking critically at advertising campaigns. Many antihunting campaigns are visible and well-funded. Wildlife agencies, on the other hand, do not necessarily spend their money on publicity programs that defend hunting.

The question of hunting is really more of an emotional and moral issue than an environmental issue. This is where your own personal belief system comes into play. The key is to consider all of the factors, and then to decide for yourself.

Hunting means taking the life of an animal, and you have to feel comfortable with that. Talk to hunters in your family or community about how they view their role. You will probably find that they have respect for the wildlife they hunt. You may also find that hunting in your area actually helps to control problems of overpopulation.

If you decide that hunting is not for you, that is okay. If friends or family expect you to hunt, you can explain to them exactly why it is not for you. Whatever your reason, people should respect your decision.

A Final Word for Young Hunters

Each hunter must assume personal responsibility for his or her sport. Hunters must always ensure that certain principles, such as fair chase, are not violated. They must be committed to obeying all season and bag limits, along with

Help for Hype

Find out the facts. Some organizations may be more reputable than others with regard to the information that they publish. (And by the way, don't believe everything you read on the Internet.)

Most of all, try not to fall into the pattern of condemning someone who disagrees with you regarding "to hunt or not to hunt." It is a complex issue and everyone has the right to his or her opinion.

all the other regulations that govern hunting. Finally, they must take an active part in helping to police their own ranks by taking a strong stand against poaching and other wildlife crime. Sportsmen and sportswomen should never be bashful about reporting those who deliberately violate the rules of their sport.

If hunters do these things and hunt responsibly, our society will continue to support hunting as a viable recreational activity.

Glossary

Action
The parts of a firearm that load and fire a gun.

Backstop
An object designed to safely stop the continued path of a projectile fired from a gun, bow, or crossbow.

Bait
Food or other enticement used to lure wild game within shooting range.

Blinds
Simple shelters used to conceal a hunter from wild game.

Bolt
Projectile fired from a crossbow.

Bow
A handheld device used to shoot arrows.

Buck Rubs
Small trees or saplings that have been shredded or scrapped by a buck's antlers.

Buckshot
Shot shells containing large shot sizes, which are used mostly for big game.

Caliber
The diameter of a bullet or the inside diameter of a rifle's barrel.

Camouflage
Materials designed to blend into a wilderness background for concealment.

Cap and Ball
A type of muzzleloading firearm ignition that involves using a primer cap, which ignites the powder charge in the muzzle.

Carryover
The number of animals a habitat can support or carry over during the winter months.

Choke
A constriction built into the end of a shotgun barrel that is designed to tighten the pattern or shot string to provide a longer effective range.

Clay Bird
A clay disk used as a target for shotgun shooting.

Crossbow
A bow fixed crosswise on a stock with a trigger release.

Driving
Method of hunting that involves using people to push wild game toward hunters in waiting.

Fair Chase
The concept of allowing game animals to have a fair chance of escape.

Flintlock

Primitive ignition system for a muzzleloading firearm that involves using a piece of flint to send a shower of sparks into a pan of priming powder to ignite the powder in the barrel of the gun.

Game

Wild animals that are hunted for food and sport.

Game Calls

Devices that produce certain sounds that attract animals.

Game Laws

Laws that regulate sport hunting and protect non-huntable species.

Game Tags

Tags that are required by wildlife agencies to place on animal carcasses.

Gauge

The method by which shotgun size and the size of a shot charge are determined.

Global Positioning System (GPS)

Handheld computers that can calculate one's exact position using a global positioning satellite.

Habitat

A place containing all the necessary requirements for a particular species of wildlife to live such as food, water, shelter, and space.

Habitat Loss

The loss of crucial wildlife habitat, usually to unrestricted human development such as housing developments, highways, or shopping malls.

Harvest

A term referring to the annual take of surplus game by hunting.

Huntable Surplus

A surplus of game animals reproduced annually during the breeding season in excess of the numbers that a habitat can support during the winter.

In-Line Muzzleloader

A modern muzzleloading rifle with the firing mechanism in direct line with the gun's barrel.

Lacy Act

A law that makes the transportation of illegally taken wildlife across state boundaries a federal felony.

Muzzleloader

A firearm that requires the powder charge and projectiles to be loaded individually by pushing them down the barrel with a ramrod.

Nonrenewable Resources

Natural resources available in fixed amounts such as coal, oil, and gas.

P-R Funds

A special excise tax levied on sporting arms and ammunition that is used for wildlife restoration and hunter education.

Ramrod

A slim rod used to drive a powder charge, patch, and projectile down the barrel of a muzzle loading firearm.

Renewable Resources

Natural resources that reproduce themselves annually, such as wildlife.

Rifle

Firearm with grooves inside the barrel to cause the projectile to spin when fired.

Riffled Slug

Single projectile ammunition for shotguns.

Safety

A blocking device that prevents the trigger from pulling or blocks the firing pin or hammer from striking a chambered shell.

Safety Harness

Safety device used to prevent a hunter from falling out of a tree.

Scrapes

Small area of earth that is scraped by the hooves of a buck during the breeding or rutting season to mark his territory.

Shot String

Shot fired from a shotgun is strung out in a line called a shot string.

Sight

Mechanism used for aiming a firearm, bow, or crossbow.

Small Game

Smaller animals such as squirrels, rabbits, grouse and pheasants.

Sporting Arm

A firearm used for the purpose of hunting or target shooting.

Stalking

Method of hunting consisting of carefully moving through the woods searching for game or following the trail of a game animal.

Stand
A place where a hunter waits for game, such as in a tree stand.

Still-Hunting
Waiting in one spot for legal game to appear.

Sustained Yield
The goal of regulated hunting. To control the harvest of game animals annually through wildlife law enforcement so each year's harvest does not exceed a wild population's ability to recover.

Topographical Map
A map that includes terrain types and elevations.

Wildlife Conservation
The philosophy of wisely using renewable natural resources.

Wildlife Management
A science of managing wildlife resources.

Resources

Organizations

In the United States

American Hunting Dog Club (AHDC)
Box 145
Cranby, CT 06035
Web site: http://users.ntplx.net/-jmfink

National Rifle Association
Hunter Services Department
11250 Waples Mill Road
Fairfax, VA 22030
Web site: http://www.nra.org

National Shooting Sports Foundation
Flintlock Ridge Office Center
11 Mile Hill Road
Newtown, CT 06470-2359
Web site: http://www.nssf.org

National Wild Turkey Federation
P.O. Box 530
Edgefield, SC 29824
Web site: http://www.nwtf.org

In Canada

Canada's Northwest Territories Explorers' Guide
Web site: http://www.nwttravel.nt.ca

Outdoor Canada
Web site: http://www.outdoor-canada.com

Canada Fishing and Hunting Outfitters
Web site: http://www.travel2canada.com/fish&hunt.htm

Web Sites

Blackpowder Hunting
http://www.barrettwebs.com/ibha/index.htm

Competition Shooting—Wheelchair Sports USA
http:// www.wsusa.org

Internet Geographic Shooting Sports
http://www.shootingsports.com/

National Skeet Shooting and Sporting Clays Association
http://nssa-nsca.com/nssa

New Shooting Games
http://users.ntplx.net/-jmfink

Sporting Clays Fact Sheet
http://www.ool.com/misc.files/sportclay.html

Women's Shooting Sports Foundation
http://www.wssf.org

For Further Reading

Books

Bauer, Erwin, and Peggy Bauer. *Big Game of North America.* Stillwater, MN: Voyageur Press, Inc., 1998.

Christian, Chris. *The Gun Digest Book of Trap and Skeet Shooting.* Iola, WI: Krause Publications, 1994.

Field & Stream: The World of Big-Game Hunting. Minnetonka, MN: Creative Publishing International, 1999.

Lawrence, H. Lea. *The Archer's and Bowhunter's Bible.* New York: Doubleday and Company, 1993.

McIntyre, Thomas. *The Field & Stream Shooting Sports Handbook.* New York: Lyons Press, 1999.

McLead-Everette, Sharon. *Walk Softly With Me: Adventures of a Woman Big-Game Guide in Alaska.* Fairbanks, AK: Vanessapress, 1998.

Migdalski Tom. *The Complete Book to Shotgunning Games.* Lincolnwood, IL: NTC Contemporary Publishing Company, 1997.

Murtz, Harold A. *The Gun Digest of Sporting Clays.* Iola, WI: Krause Publications, 1999.

Painter, Doug Hunting. *The Field & Stream Firearms Safety Handbook.* New York: Lyons Press, 1999.

Valerio, Maurizio. *Big Game Hunting in North America.* Baker City, OR: Picked-By-You Guides, 1999.

Magazines

Blackpowder Hunting

Field & Stream

Outdoor Life

Fur, Fish and Game

Deer and Deer Hunting

Index

A

ammunition, 15, 17–18, 22, 31
animal rights organizations, 47–48
archery, 31, 43
archery hunting, 29

B

backstop, 17, 42
bait, 28
bears, 10, 28, 29
beginner, 14, 36
blinds, 28
boots, 19–20

C

caliber, 16–17
calling, 5, 25–26
caribou, 13
clothing, 19–20, 22
compass, 21
coyotes, 25
crows, 25

D

deer, 9, 14, 23, 25, 26, 27, 28, 29
driving game, 27
ducks, 13

E

elk, 10, 13, 25, 26

F

fair chase, 7, 30, 51
firearms, 14, 15–17, 22, 35
firearm safety, 31, 33, 35–36
foxes, 25

G

gauge, 16–17
geese, 13, 25
global positioning system (GPS), 21

H

hunter education, 21, 31–32, 35, 41
hunter safety, 31, 32–34
hunting
    history of, 8–10
    precautions to take, 40
    pros and cons, 47–49, 51
    skills required, 7
hunting dogs, 29
hunting license, 21

K

knife, 19

M

maps, 21
mentoring, 36
moose, 13, 25
muzzle loading, 29, 31

N

National Rifle Association, 42, 46
National Wild Turkey Association, 46

P

poaching, 51
purchasing a firearm, 35

R

research, 38
rifle, 15–17

S

safety, 27, 31–34
scouting, 23, 26
shotgun, 15, 16–17
sport hunting, 10, 12–14
sportsmen, 10–14
sportsmen clubs, 32, 42, 46
stand hunting, 26–27
state wildlife agencies, 10, 12, 21, 31, 32, 38
survival kit, 23

T

target practice, 41, 42
target practice competitions
    archery, 43
    high power rifle, 42
    muzzle loader or black
        powder, 43
    small bore rifle, 42
trap and skeet shooting, 44–45
tree stand safety, 32, 24
turkeys, 6, 28

U

U.S. Fish and Wildlife Service, 12

W

waterfowl, 10, 12, 28
wildlife, 4–7, 8, 9, 10, 12–14, 24, 30, 48
wildlife management, 12

Y

Youth Field Day, 46
Youth Hunter Education Challenge, 46

Credits

About the Author

Jack Weaver is a graduate of the Pennsylvania Game Commission's Ross Leffler School of Conservation. He has served as a wildlife conservation officer for the Pennsylvania Game Commission (PGC) since 1969. He has written extensively for the PGC's official magazine, *Pennsylvania Game News,* and is also the author of *Phantoms Of The Woods.* He spent the last six years of his career as the information and education supervisor for PGC's northeast region. Throughout his career, Mr. Weaver worked extensively with Pennsylvania's Hunter Education Program. He retired from the Pennsylvania Game Commission in 1999.

Photo Credits

Series Design

Oliver H. Rosenberg

Layout

Cynthia Williamson